FOUR FL
THE INDIGENOUS PEOPLE OF GREAT BRITAIN

DNA, History and the Right to Existence of the Native Inhabitants of the British Isles

By Arthur Kemp
B.A. (Pol. Sci, Int. Pol., Pub. Ad.)

Ostara Publications

FOUR FLAGS: THE INDIGENOUS PEOPLE OF GREAT BRITAIN
DNA, History and the Right to Existence of the Native
Inhabitants of the British Isles

By Arthur Kemp

First edition January 2010
This edition December 2011

Ostara Publications
Box 671
Burlingont
IA 52601-0671
United States of America

ISBN 978-1-4452-8775-1

Table of Contents

Section One: *Introduction* 1

Section Two: *Indigenous People — A Definition* 3

Section Three: *Haplogroups and the Identification of Peoples* 10

Section Four: *Haplogroups Found in Britain (Prior to Modern Third World Immigration)* 16

Section Five: *A History of the Populating of Britain* 26

Section Six: *The Rights of the Indigenous People of Britain* 42

Bibliography 50

Index 52

Also by Arthur Kemp:

March of the Titans: The Complete History of the White Race

The Immigration Invasion: How Third World Immigration is Destroying the First World and What Must be done to Stop it.

Jihad: Islam's 1,300 Year War on Western Civilisation

Folk and Nation: Underpinning the Ethnostate

Victory or Violence: The Story of the AWB of South Africa

The Lie of Apartheid and Other True Stories from Southern Africa

Available at www.ostarapublications.com

Section One: *Introduction*

IN April 2009, more than 122 Members of Parliament at Westminster signed a declaration which affirmed that there was no such thing as an indigenous people in Britain.
  This declaration by members of the Conservative, Liberal-Democrat and Labour parties said that there was no such thing as a native people of Britain, implying that all were foreigners and thereby justifying the current immigration invasion.
  This astonishing declaration, which took the form of an Early Day Motion entitled the "Rights of Tribal and Indigenous Peoples", noted the Government's refusal to put the rights of indigenous peoples on a legal footing with regard to protection against "climate change." The reason why the Government had refused to "put these rights on a firm legal footing" was, the declaration said, done "on the grounds that there are no indigenous peoples in the United Kingdom."
  The declaration went on to say that this absence of an indigenous people of Britain was no reason not to worry about indigenous people elsewhere, pointing out that "this has not prevented either the Netherlands or Spain from joining the list of 20 countries, including Brazil," from doing so because "protecting the rights of indigenous peoples is a matter of international concern."
  Not one MP, not one newspaper, not one environmental group, raised their objection to this blanking out of the concept of an indigenous people of Britain.
  Yet there are indigenous people of Britain: the Scots, the Welsh, the Irish and the English. All have their own defined identities, traditions and culture, and even though they have often been in conflict with one another, together they created one of the mightiest nations of modern times: Great Britain.
  This is the story of the indigenous people of Britain: who they are, how they came about, their history and heritage.

Genocide

  The word genocide literally means the "death of genes." This work will also show that there is a clear genetic basis to the indigenous people of Britain as well. The declaration by the Conservative, Liberal-Democrat and Labour parties that there are no indigenous people in Britain is nothing short of academic genocide. It is the wiping out of the historical record in preparation and justification for the wiping out of the indigenous people of Britain through mass Third World immigration.

Here, then, is the historical and DNA record which proves the existence of the indigenous people of Britain — and their right to exist as a free and sovereign nation along with every other indigenous people on earth.

Section Two: *Indigenous People — A Definition*

ACCORDING to the United Nations' Department of Economic and Social Affairs, as prepared in their policy document "The Concept of Indigenous Peoples," a background paper prepared by the Secretariat of the Permanent Forum on Indigenous Issues", and issued in January 2004, the following are characteristics of an indigenous people:

"Indigenous communities, peoples and nations are those which, having a historical continuity with pre-invasion and pre-colonial societies that developed on their territories, consider themselves distinct from other sectors of the societies now prevailing on those territories, or parts of them.

"They form at present non-dominant sectors of society and are determined to preserve, develop and transmit to future generations their ancestral territories, and their ethnic identity, as the basis of their continued existence as peoples, in accordance with their own cultural patterns, social institutions and legal system.

"This historical continuity may consist of the continuation, for an extended period reaching into the present of one or more of the following factors:

a) Occupation of ancestral lands, or at least of part of them;
b) Common ancestry with the original occupants of these lands;
c) Culture in general, or in specific manifestations (such as religion, living under a tribal system, membership of an indigenous community, dress, means of livelihood, lifestyle, etc.);
d) Language (whether used as the only language, as mother-tongue, as the habitual means of communication at home or in the family, or as the main, preferred, habitual, general or normal language);
e) Residence in certain parts of the country, or in certain regions of the world;
f) Other relevant factors.

"On an individual basis, an indigenous person is one who belongs to these indigenous populations through self-identification as indigenous (group consciousness) and is recognized and accepted by these populations as one of its members (acceptance by the group).

"This preserves for these communities the sovereign right and power to decide who belongs to them, without external interference."

UN Declaration on the Rights of Indigenous Peoples

The Draft Declaration on the Rights of Indigenous Peoples of the United Nations states that "Indigenous peoples have the collective and individual right to maintain and develop their distinct identities and characteristics, including the right to identify themselves as indigenous and to be recognized as such (article 8) and Indigenous peoples have the collective right to determine their own citizenship in accordance with their customs and traditions.

"Indigenous citizenship does not impair the right of indigenous individuals to obtain citizenship of the States in which they live (art. 32)."

ILO Definition of Indigenous Peoples

The definition of indigenous peoples as used in the International Labour Organisation Convention No. 169, concerning the working rights of indigenous and tribal peoples, states that the term can be applied to "tribal peoples whose social, cultural and economic conditions distinguish them from other sections of the national community and whose status is regulated wholly or partially by their own customs or traditions or by special laws or regulations and to peoples who are regarded as indigenous on account of their descent from the populations which inhabit the country at the time of conquest or colonisation."

World Bank Definition of Indigenous Peoples

The World Bank also has a definition of indigenous people. According to its Operational Directive 4.20, 1991, an indigenous people can "be identified in particular geographical areas by the presence in varying degrees of the following characteristics:

a) close attachment to ancestral territories and to the natural resources in these areas;
b) self-identification and identification by others as members of a distinct cultural group;
c) an indigenous language, often different from the national language;
d) presence of customary social and political institutions; and
e) primarily subsistence-oriented production."

Section Two: Indigenous People — A Definition

The Three Common Factors in Defining an Indigenous People

From these definitions, three things stand out as common factors:
- Firstly, there must be a provable and historical continuous link between an indigenous people and a landmass;
- Secondly, the indigenous people must have a large degree of homogeneity in ethnic origin, race and culture; and
- Thirdly, there is usually an element of colonisation by foreign peoples involved. Generally speaking, this involves the mass transfer of people of different ethnic or racial origin to the lands traditionally occupied by the indigenous peoples.

This occurs to the point where such colonists form a substantial part of the population and deny the indigenous people their rights in their own territory. This includes forcing foreign cultures, traditions and ways of life upon the indigenous people so that their native culture is placed under threat or even extermination.

European Colonisation and Indigenous Peoples

Traditionally, the definition of indigenous peoples was usually only applied to inhabitants of the Third World who had suffered colonisation at the hands of European powers. This process occurred largely during the era of European exploration and discovery.

In this way, Europeans "discovered" the Far East, the Australias, Sub-Saharan Africa and the Americas.

In each of those land masses, the indigenous peoples were subjected to varying degrees of colonisation. In some regions, such as South America, the majority of the local indigenous cultures were completely destroyed though military conquest (apart from isolated tribes deep in the Amazon jungle). The ethnic and racial homogeneity of those peoples was disrupted through mixing with the colonisers and large numbers of imported African slaves. The latter process is particularly noticeable in Brazil and parts of Mexico.

In the North Americas, the indigenous population was also militarily defeated and displaced, eventually ending up in "Indian reservations" where the European colonisers were forbidden from acquiring further land.

Canada recently (1999) created the largest federal territory of Nunavut (which is the size of Western Europe) out of the Northwest Territories to accommodate the demands of the Inuit indigenous people for self-government.

In Africa, European colonists divided up most of the continent as directly ruled colonies, sending large numbers of their populations out to settle those lands.

In contrast with the Australias, however, conflict with the natives of African lands did not result in the displacement of the indigenous people. This ultimately resulted in colonial rule over the local population collapsing though sheer weight of numbers, with the European colonial powers unable to militarily contain rising African resentment at being governed by Europeans.

This led to the decolonisation process after World War II, the final chapter of which can be said to have been written with the introduction of an African majority government in South Africa in 1994.

As mentioned, the colonisation of the Australias followed a remarkably different path to that of Africa. Like their cousins in North America, the European colonists arranged their settlement of Australia in such a way that they became the majority population, effectively displacing the indigenous population.

Non-European Colonisation and Indigenous Peoples

The liberal focus on Third World peoples being the subjects of European colonisation has deliberately ignored the reality that non-European powers also colonised other peoples in ancient and early modern times.

The great expansions of the Mongols under Genghis Khan and his successors, for example, saw many Asiatic tribes conquered, destroyed or assimilated in their march across the Steppes.

Other important (but ignored by the liberal media and academia) non-European colonisation programmes included:
- the Nubian conquests of Ancient Egypt;
- the Persian conquests of vast areas in the Middle East;
- the Muslim conquests of the Middle East, North Africa and parts of southern Europe;
- the Muslim Ottoman Turkish conquest of south eastern Europe; and
- in modern times, the colonisation of Tibet by the Han Chinese.

All of these colonial conquests resulted in either the displacement or destruction of indigenous peoples whose ancestral lands lay in the paths of the conquering powers.

The important lesson of colonialism is, however, that it was not just Europe which colonised the Third World, but that colonisation and the displacement of indigenous peoples is something which has happened to almost all peoples of all races at one time or another throughout history.

The United Nations Declaration on the Rights of Indigenous Peoples

The preamble to the United Nations Declaration on the Rights of Indigenous Peoples, adopted by the General Assembly Resolution 61/295 on 13 September 2007, makes a number of important statements.

They include the following:
"Indigenous peoples are equal to all other peoples, while recognizing the right of all peoples to be different, to consider themselves different, and to be respected as such,
"Affirming also that all peoples contribute to the diversity and richness of civilizations and cultures, which constitute the common heritage of humankind,
"Concerned that indigenous peoples have suffered from historic injustices as a result of, inter alia, their colonization and dispossession of their lands, territories and resources, thus preventing them from exercising, in particular, their right to development in accordance with their own needs and interests,
"Recognizing the urgent need to respect and promote the inherent rights of indigenous peoples which derive from their political, economic and social structures and from their cultures, spiritual traditions, histories and philosophies, especially their rights to their lands, territories and resources,
"Welcoming the fact that indigenous peoples are organizing themselves for political, economic, social and cultural enhancement and in order to bring to an end all forms of discrimination and oppression wherever they occur."
The Declaration goes on to state that indigenous peoples have the following inalienable rights:
"Article 3
Indigenous peoples have the right to self-determination. By virtue of that right they freely determine their political status and freely pursue their economic, social and cultural development.
Article 5
Indigenous peoples have the right to maintain and strengthen their distinct political, legal, economic, social and cultural institutions, while retaining their right to participate fully, if

they so choose, in the political, economic, social and cultural life of the State.

Article 8

1. Indigenous peoples and individuals have the right not to be subjected to forced assimilation or destruction of their culture.
2. States shall provide effective mechanisms for prevention of, and redress for:
(a) Any action which has the aim or effect of depriving them of their integrity as distinct peoples, or of their cultural values or ethnic identities;
(b) Any action which has the aim or effect of dispossessing them of their lands, territories or resources;
(c) Any form of forced population transfer which has the aim or effect of violating or undermining any of their rights;
(d) Any form of forced assimilation or integration;
(e) Any form of propaganda designed to promote or incite racial or ethnic discrimination directed against them.

Article 10

Indigenous peoples shall not be forcibly removed from their lands or territories. No relocation shall take place without the free, prior and informed consent of the indigenous peoples concerned and after agreement on just and fair compensation and, where possible, with the option of return.

Article 11

1. Indigenous peoples have the right to practise and revitalize their cultural traditions and customs. This includes the right to maintain, protect and develop the past, present and future manifestations of their cultures, such as archaeological and historical sites, artefacts, designs, ceremonies, technologies and visual and performing arts and literature.
2. States shall provide redress through effective mechanisms, which may include restitution, developed in conjunction with indigenous peoples, with respect to their cultural, intellectual, religious and spiritual property taken without their free, prior and informed consent or in violation of their laws, traditions and customs.

Article 15

1. Indigenous peoples have the right to the dignity and diversity of their cultures, traditions, histories and aspirations which shall be appropriately reflected in education and public information.
2. States shall take effective measures, in consultation and cooperation with the indigenous peoples concerned, to combat prejudice and eliminate discrimination and to promote tolerance,

Section Two: Indigenous People — A Definition

understanding and good relations among indigenous peoples and all other segments of society."

The Indigenous People of the British Isles

It is the contention of this work that the people known to history as the Scots, the Welsh, the Irish and the English, who together form the people of the British Isles, qualify as an indigenous people.

They form an ethnically homogenous unit, share a genetically-proven common racial heritage, have a link to a defined land mass going back thousands of years and, most importantly, are currently being colonised through mass Third World immigration which is denying them many of the rights stipulated in the UN Declaration on the Rights of Indigenous Peoples.

If it can be shown — and this work will — that the native people of the British Isles fulfil all the criteria for an indigenous people, then there is no legal or moral reason why their rights to territorial integrity, cultural uniformity and ethnic homogeneity cannot be enforced.

Section Three: *Haplogroups and the Identification of Peoples*

MODERN genetic research has enabled scientists to map out markers which can clearly identify different groups within modern humans.

It is the study of Deoxyribonucleic acid, or DNA, a nucleic acid that contains the genetic instructions used in the development and functioning of all known living organisms, which has allowed this dramatic breakthrough.

DNA is arranged into structures called chromosomes which are in turn divided into three groups: Y-chromosomes; X-Chromosomes; and Autosomal DNA.

People normally have 23 pairs of chromosomes, or 46 chromosomes in total. Twenty two of these pairs (44 chromosomes) are Autosomal DNA, or "non-sex" chromosomes found in the DNA nucleus.

The 23rd pair of chromosomes contains the "sex chromosomes" (called Y for males, X for females) which determine the human's sex.

Autosomal DNA is inherited from both parents and controls physical characteristics such as eye colour and physical appearance, or what is popularly called "race."

A male individual's patrilineal lineage can be traced using his Y chromosomes because the Y chromosome passes down unchanged from father to son. Because this Y-chromosome is passed down unchanged from one generation to the next, it can show a vast amount of information about the ancestors of that particular person.

Female ancestry is determined by Mitochondrial DNA (mtDNA). In humans, mtDNA is passed from mother to daughter unchanged, in the same way that Y-Chromosomes are passed down from father to son. An mtDNA profile will determine to which "group" that person belongs.

Y-Chromosomes and mtDNA Put into Haplogroups

In order to facilitate the understanding of how this genetic clustering works, scientists have classed all the different genetic components into ancestral clans, called "haplogroups." Letters of the alphabet have been assigned to the haplogroups for differentiation purposes and in order to represent the branches of the tree for Homo sapiens. The

Section Three: Haplogroups and the Identification of Peoples

study of haplogroups therefore provides modern scientists with the key to understanding human origins going back thousands of years.

In this way, each major branch of the Homo sapiens family has been assigned a haplogroup, or in most cases, a dominant haplogroup. Furthermore, testing of "base" populations (that is, "indigenous" populations associated with specific areas has provided scientists with specific clusters for specific people.

A modern DNA test will, therefore, be able to determine the ultimate origin of an individual. This science is already being used by law enforcement agencies across the world to identify crime victims or criminals.

By comparing DNA samples to these "base" population records, it is possible to determine an individual's precise "group" origin and link them back to a specific geographic area, no matter how long they might have lived in another region.

Y Haplogroup Categories

A "haplotype" is the genetic make-up of an individual chromosome. By analysing haplotypes, the specific geographic areas of origin of that haplotype can be identified. Some examples will suffice:

In the Y-Haplogroup categories, someone showing the "A" Y-Chromosome marker is representative of peoples from Sub-Saharan Africa. Defined by the further marker called "M91," many individuals carrying this live in Ethiopia, the Sudan and southern regions in Africa.

Marker M60 defines Haplogroup B, another ancient African lineage with a broad dispersal across that continent.

Marker M130 origin people are found throughout mainland Asia, the South Pacific, and at low frequency in Native American populations. This marker gave rise to Haplogroup C in southern Asia which in turn spread through New Guinea, Australia, and northern Asia and is currently found in large numbers in India.

Haplogroup D is found primarily in central Asia, southeast Asia and in Japan. Haplogroup D2, or marker M174, is found exclusively in Japan.

The E3a Haplogroup is from sub-Saharan Africa and is the most common lineage amongst blacks in America, indicating that was the major source of the African slave trade during early colonial times.

There are a great many other haplogroups (see the haplogroup charts) all of which indicate precise national origins and form the basis of modern identifying populations.

The Implications of Haplogroups and Their Geographic Origins

The close correlation between haplotypes and geographic areas is an important determinant in identifying which population is "native," or indigenous to a specific area.

All of the currently accepted Third World indigenous peoples are represented by specific haplogroups.

If it can be shown that Britain (or any of the European nations) also has specific unique haplogroups which have been established in distinct regions, then there is no historical, genetic or legal reason why the populations who have been resident in these areas for thousands of years cannot also qualify for "indigenous" status.

All that remains, therefore, is to correlate the historical record of the British Isles with the latest DNA results. If they match up, the case for the existence of an indigenous people is proven.

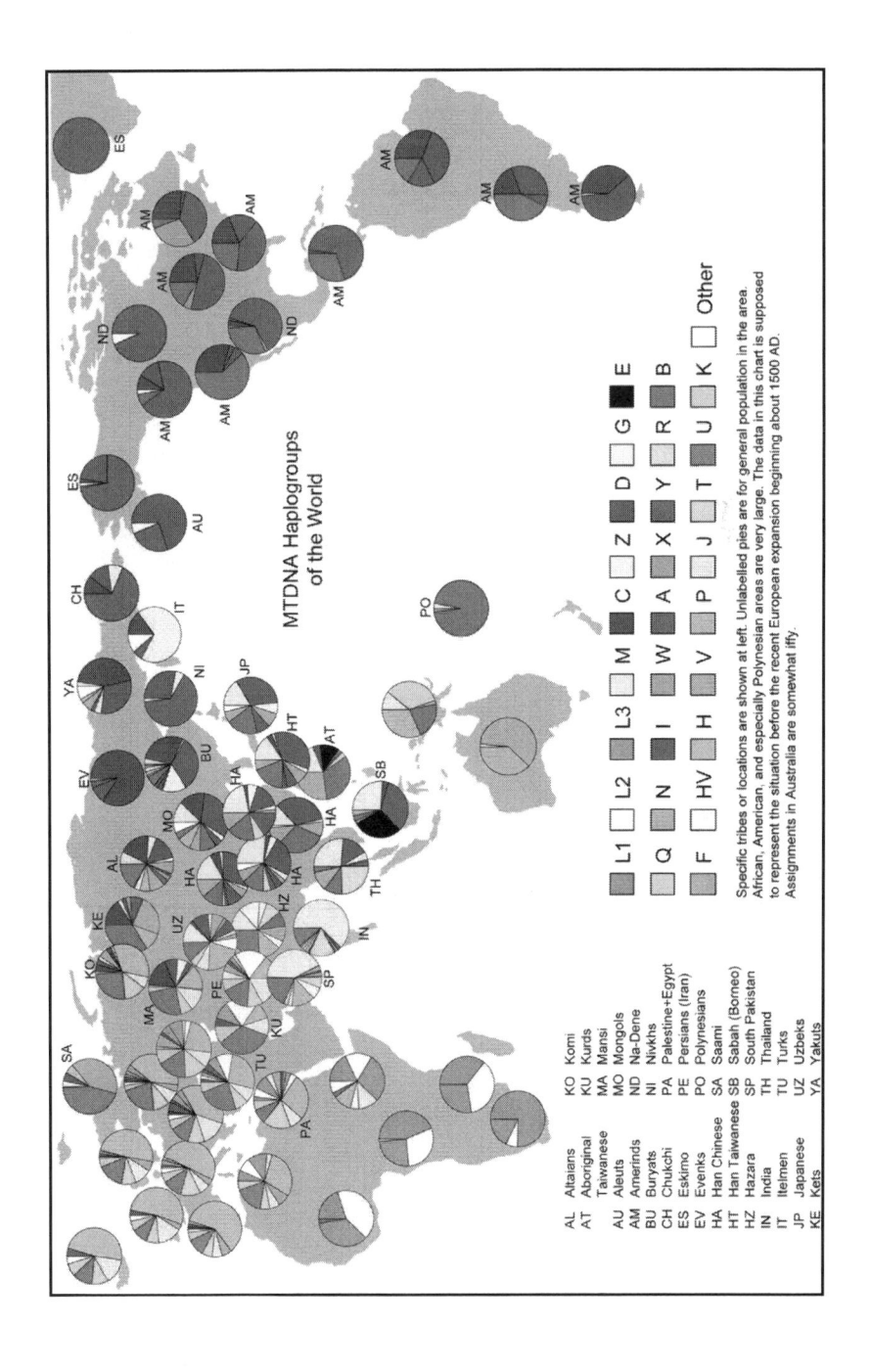

Section Three: Haplogroups and the Identification of Peoples

MTDNA Haplogroups of the World

L1	L2	L3	M	C	Z	D	G	E
Q	N	I	W	A	X	Y	R	B
F		HV	H	V	P	J	T	U	K	Other

Specific tribes or locations are shown at left. Unlabelled pies are for general population in the area. African, American, and especially Polynesian areas are very large. The data in this chart is supposed to represent the situation before the recent European expansion beginning about 1500 AD. Assignments in Australia are somewhat iffy.

AL	Altaians	KO	Komi
AT	Aboriginal Taiwanese	KU	Kurds
		MA	Mansi
AU	Aleuts	MO	Mongols
AM	Amerinds	ND	Na-Dene
BU	Buryats	NI	Nivkhs
CH	Chukchi	PA	Palestine+Egypt
ES	Eskimo	PE	Persians (Iran)
EV	Evenks	PO	Polynesians
HA	Han Chinese	SA	Saami
HT	Han Taiwanese	SB	Sabah (Borneo)
HZ	Hazara	SP	South Pakistan
IN	India	TH	Thailand
IT	Itelmen	TU	Turks
JP	Japanese	UZ	Uzbeks
KE	Kets	YA	Yakuts

13

Four Flags: The Indigenous People of Britain

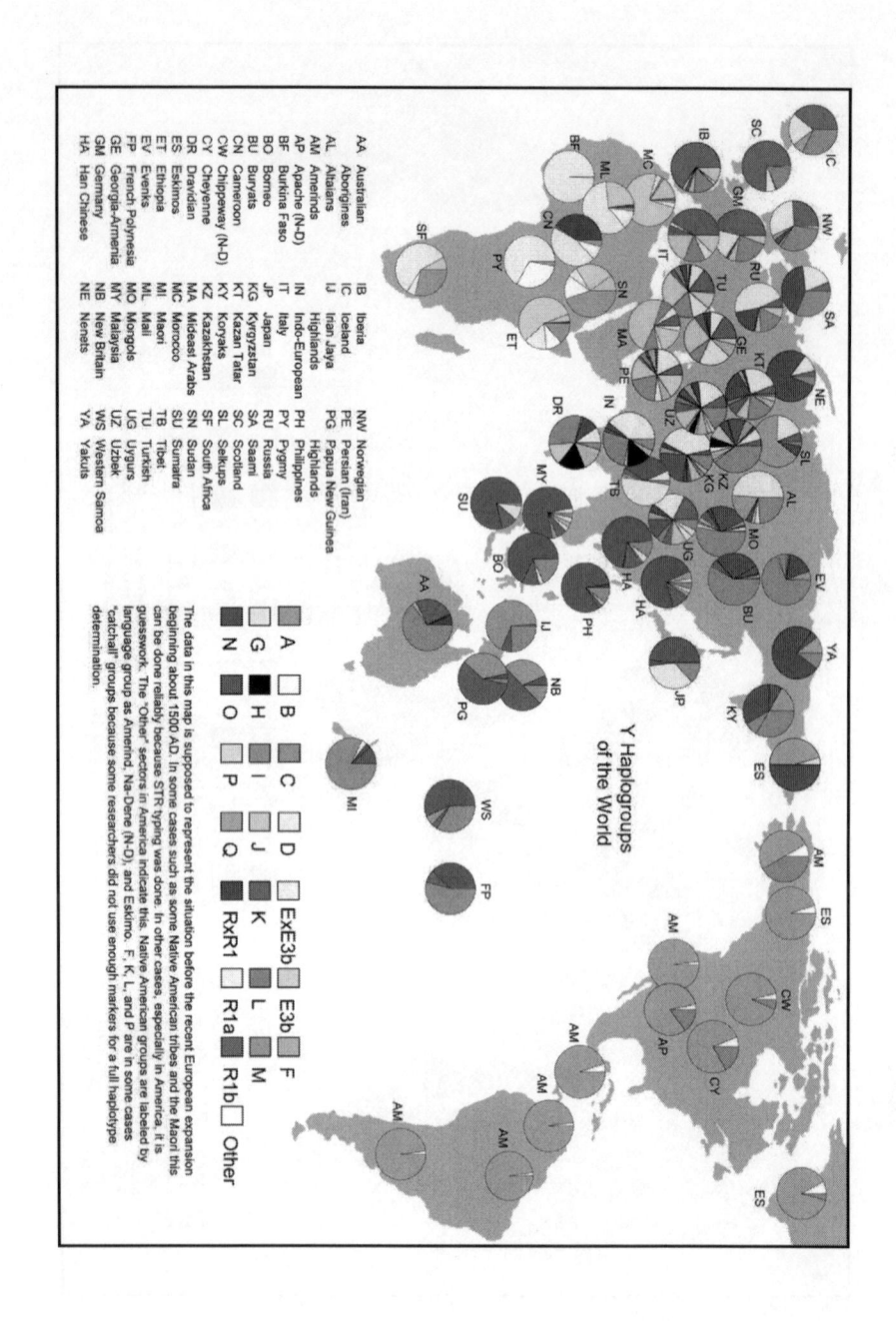

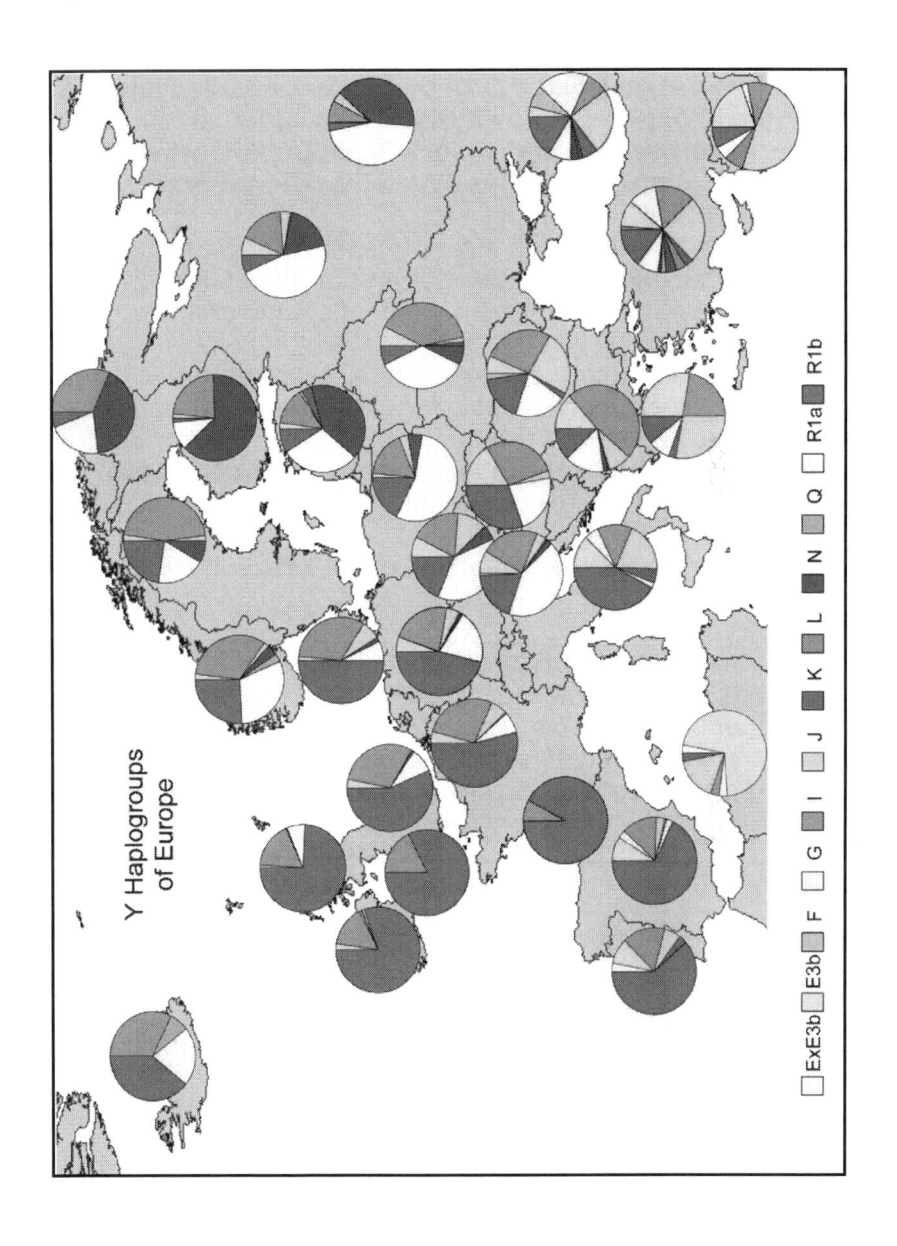

Section Three: Haplogroups and the Identification of Peoples

Y Haplogroups of Europe

ExE3b E3b F G I J K L N Q R1a R1b

Section Four: *Haplogroups Found in Britain (Prior to Modern Third World Immigration)*

THE advent of developed DNA testing has enabled forensic scientists, geneticists and historians alike to lay out a highly accurate map of the world's population prior to the mass migrations of peoples which marked the start of the colonial period.

The British Isles are no exception, and the Y-Chromosome and mtDNA ancestry of our homeland has been thoroughly mapped in a large number of scientific works (listed as Appendix 1).

The results of this research have revealed that, genetically speaking, the population native to the British Isles is closely associated with the larger region of Western Europe and in particular with the following haplotypes (note: all data is from samples prior to current Third World immigration):

Y-Chromosome Haplotypes Found in Britain

R1b1 (R1b1b2)

The R1b1 Haplotype (also known until recently as R1b) is the most common haplogroup in Britain. It forms 67 percent of the population in England, 72.5 percent in Scotland, 82 percent in Wales and 79 percent in Ireland.

This averages out across all of Britain (excluding Ireland) to nearly 74 percent of the male population having a common origin — a remarkable degree of homogeneity. The implications for Ireland are also apparent.

The R1b1 Haplotype has a number of mutations, or subgroups, known as "subclades." These subclades are identified by the addition of numbers and letters to the R1 base haplogroup title. The major R1 subclade present in Britain is known as R1b1b2, which distinguishes the population of the British Isles from most other R1b variants.

Y Haplogroups off the British Isles.

Section Four: Haplogroups Found in Britain

Frequencies of Y-Chromosome Haplogroups in the British Isles Expressed in Percentages

Region/Haplogroup	I1	I2a	I2b	R1a	R1b	G2a	J2	E1b1b	T (+ L)	Q
England	14	2.5	4.5	4.5	67	1.5	3.5	2	0.5	0.5
Scotland	9	1	4	8.5	72.5	0.5	2	1.5	0.5	0.5
Wales	6	0.5	1	2	82	4	1.5	2	1	0
Ireland	7	2	4	3	79	1	1.5	2	0	0

Frequencies of mtDNA Haplogroups in the British Isles Expressed in Percentages

Region/Haplogroup	H	H1 +H3	V	J	T	U	U2	U3	U4	U5	K	I	W	X2	Other
England	42	6.5	3.5	9	11	14	0.5	0	3	8	9.5	3.5	2	1.5	4
Scotland	42.5	3.5	3.5	14	11.5	13	1.5	1	2.5	7	6.5	5	1	1.5	1.5
Wales	43		1.5	9.5	11	10	0.5	0.5	0.5	4.5	9.5	6	0	1	7.5
Ireland	38.5	11	4	10	12	13	2	0.5	2.5	6	11	3	2.5	1.5	4.5

17

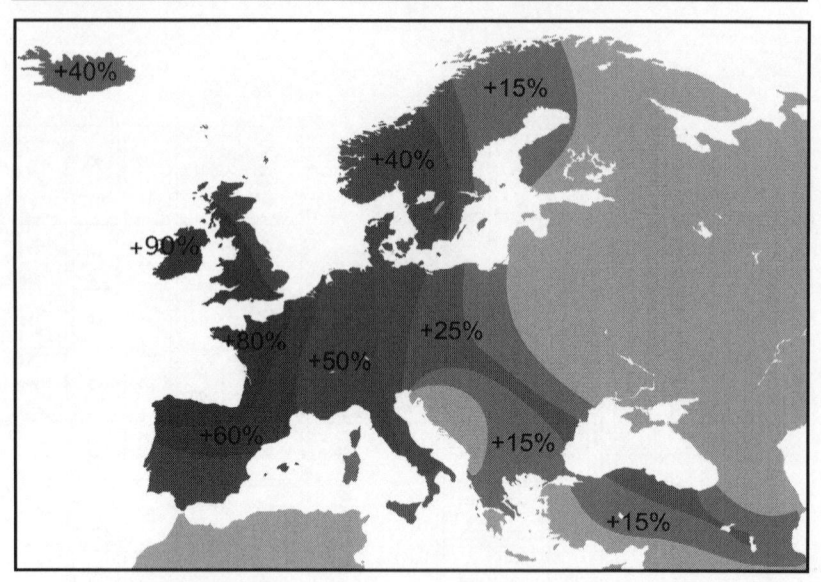

Distribution of the R1b Y-Chromosome haplogroup, expressed as a percentage of the total Y-Chromosomes in each region.

DNA sequences which appear frequently within a subclade are called "Short Tandem Repeat," or STR. The most common STR within the R1b1b2 subclade is in turn known as the Atlantic Modal Haplotype (AMH).

The AMH has six distinct genetic markers found at high frequencies in people in Wales, Ireland, and the Orkney Islands. This has been associated with the cultural grouping known as the Celtic peoples.

Further subclades of the R1b Haplotype, their age, and location are outlined below.

R1b Subclade — Date of Origin — Place of highest frequency
R1b1b2a1a1 — 1,800 years before present (ybp) — Southern England
R1b1b2a1a3 — 1,800 ybp — Southern and eastern England
R1b1b2a1b3 — 2,850 ybp — Cornwall, Wales
R1b1b2a1b4a — 2,500 ybp — England
R1b1b2a1b4c — 2,500 ybp — Mainland Britain, Ireland
R1b1b2a1b4c1/c2 — 1,800 ybp — England
R1b1b2a1b5 — 3,500 ybp — Scotland
R1b1b2a1b6 — 4,000 ybp — Ireland, mainland Britain
R1b1b2a1b6a — 3,000 ybp — Ireland, mainland Britain
R1b1b2a1b6b — 3,000 ybp — Northwest Ireland and west Scotland

(For statistical purposes, all these subclades can be classed as related because the mutated differences are quite small.)

Section Four: Haplogroups Found in Britain

R1a

Haplogroup R1a is present in Europe almost exclusively in the form of its subclade R1a1a. R1a is the third most common Y-DNA haplogroup in England.

It apparently originated in central or eastern Europe, and most likely came to England with the Germanics ("Anglo-Saxons") who settled during the seventh and eighth centuries A.D.

R1a appears at 4.5 percent in England, 8.5 percent in Scotland, 2 percent in Wales and 3 percent in Ireland.

For all of Britain (excluding Ireland) then, the Germanic "Anglo-Saxon" gene averages out at 5 percent.

I

Haplogroup I, in its variants I1, I1a and I2b, is nearly completely restricted to northwestern Europe. Those variants are most commonly associated with Viking populations and settlements.

The level of this marker in any population serves as a precise indicator of the size and presence of a Viking colony in an area. This is the likely origin of these markers in modern Britain.

- I1 runs at 14 percent in England, 9 percent in Scotland, 6 percent in Wales and 7 percent in Ireland.

GENETIC SIMILARITIES BETWEEN R1a AND R1b1

The clear genetic similarities between the R1a and R1b1 haplotypes have led scientists to conclude that both are descended from a common ancestral group who moved into Europe starting some 30,000 ybp. This was at the height of the last ice age, and at this time it appears that the ancestors of R1b1 and R1a were separated at opposite ends of Europe due to the glaciers which still held much of Europe in their grip. As a result, R1b1 became concentrated on the western side of Europe, while R1a was concentrated in the east, most notably in what is now the Ukraine. About 6000 ybp, the R1a group began migrating west into Europe. This migration became known as the "Indo-European" expansion because of the dominance of their language form. Almost all modern European languages are Indo-European in origin (with a tiny number of exceptions). *For statistical purposes, therefore, it could be justified to count the R1a and R1b1 groups as one, which would push the British homogeneity levels to nearly 80 percent.*

- I2a runs at 2.5 percent in England, 1 percent in Scotland, 0.5 percent in Wales and 2 percent in Ireland.
- I2b runs at 4.5 percent in England, 4 percent in Scotland, 1 percent in Wales and 4 percent in Ireland.
- When all of these subclades are combined for Britain (excluding Ireland), it shows that the average contribution across the entire country of the "Viking" gene runs at 4.6 percent.

* This figure could be even lower. One subclade of Haplogroup I-M436, called I-M284, has been found almost exclusively among the British, which suggests that it has been there longer than the time of the Viking incrusion into Britain.

E1b1b (E3b)

Haplogroup E1b1b (previously known as E3b) moved into southern Europe via the Middle East during Neolithic times around 9,000 years ago. E1b1b is found at 2 percent in England, 1.5 percent in Scotland, 2 percent in Wales and 2 percent in Ireland.

An average for all of Britain (excluding Ireland) for the E1b1b Y-Chromosome is therefore 1.8 percent, clustered in parts of England and northern Wales. Scientists believe that this is linked to Roman settlers or soldiers who were stationed in Britain during the years 100–300 A.D.

Another DNA study (Capelli, et al.) indicated that the E3b component could have resulted from Phoenician traders, Iberian sailors, Norman administrators or Flemish merchants of Portuguese Sephardic Jewish ancestry.

J

Haplogroup J originated in the ancient Near East and was carried into North Africa, Europe, Central Asia, Pakistan and India during the expansion of agriculture during the Neolithic period. As a result, Haplogroup J appears in Europe in decreasing frequency from west to east, and is concentrated in the south towards the Middle East.

One of its subclades, J2, occurs in Britain at the rate of 3.5 percent in England, 2 percent in Scotland, 1.5 percent in Wales and 1.5 percent in Ireland. An average occurrence in Britain (excluding Ireland) is therefore 2.3 percent, just below the average 3 percent which occurs on the northwest Atlantic European coast.

Some studies have suggested a Neolithic peopling origin for the Haplogroup J in Britain, while others have suggested (a

Section Four: Haplogroups Found in Britain

more likely explanation) a link to the Roman settlement of Britain. Evidence of this Roman link lies in the fact that it appears to parallel the E3B frequencies. Levels of J2 which range from 4 to 6 percent are also found in exactly the same areas that showed E3b, namely the former Roman settlements of Faversham, Southwell and Uttoxeter.

G

Haplotype G is represented in Britain by subclades G2a and G2a3b1. It is concentrated in Wales. The frequencies are as follows: England 1.5 percent, Scotland 0.5 percent, Wales 4 percent and Ireland 1 percent. For all of Britain then, excluding Ireland, the average of this haplotype is 2 percent.

Studies indicate that Haplogroup G expanded from the Middle East to Europe via the Black Sea and to the western Mediterranean about 5,000 ybp, running at around 4 percent of the total European population.

A clearly definable split in mutations between southern and northern Europe occurred only a few hundred years ago. Further research is necessary before this is fully understood.

T

Haplogroup T appears in tiny numbers in the British Isles, running at 0.5 percent in England, 0.5 percent in Scotland and 1 percent in Wales. It is not found in Ireland in any statistically significant numbers.

This haplotype originated in the Middle East and is still concentrated there. Its presence in Britain is most likely due to a Neolithic incursion at the end of the last ice age from Iberia, where it is also found in low numbers.

Q

Haplogroup Q is most commonly associated with an origin in Central Asia or Siberia some 15,000 to 20,000 years ago. It runs at 0.5 percent in England, 0.5 percent in Scotland and does not appear in Wales or Ireland in any numbers to be statistically significant.

Recent studies have linked the Q Haplogroup to a Turkic population which in turn is linked to a minority of Jewish males (5 percent). This may indicate the origin of the haplogroup in Britain, or it could be linked to other colonial-era migrations.

Four Flags: The Indigenous People of Britain

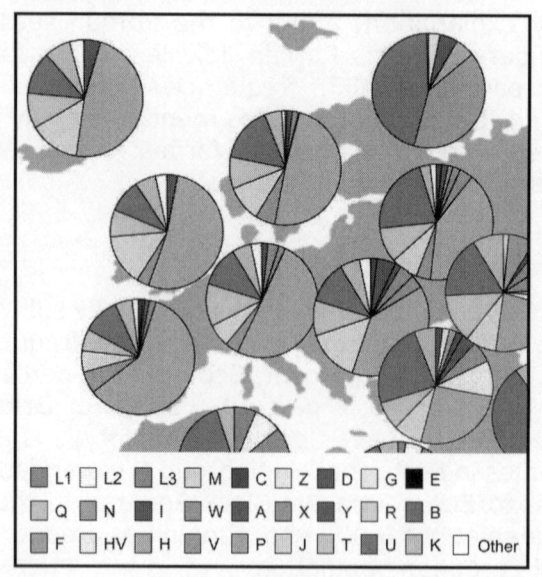

mtDNA haplogroups of Europe. Frequencies of the different female-descended chromosomes tend to be more evenly spread throughout Europe. This is because migrations were usually male-dominated undertakings. The mtDNA lines therefore tend to be older and longer established than the European male lines. Some of the most recent research has indicated that the majority of male lineages in Europe entered the Continent after the end of the last ice age.

mtDNA Haplotypes Found in Britain

Female lines tend to be more evenly spread throughout Europe, most likely because female populations tended to be more settled and less migratory than bands of males. The reasons for this are varied: the traditional role of childrearing, house making and physical strength may all have played a role.

The difference between Y-Chromosome and mtDNA Chromosome patterns is explained by the predominantly male migration pattern.

A January 2010 study (Balaresque et.al.) found that the R1b1b Y Chromosome first entered the continent some 10,000 years ago, carried by farmers who possibly originated in the Middle East.

In contrast, the maternal genetic lineages (mtDNA) seem to descend from the Palaeolithic hunter gatherers. This implies that the female lines in modern Europe are even older than the majority of male lines, while confirming the post-ice age repopulation of Europe. As a result, the mtDNA map of Britain

Section Four: Haplogroups Found in Britain

is far closer to the rest of Europe than the Y-Chromosome map.

H

Haplogroup H is by far the most common mtDNA found in Europe, accounting for anywhere between 40 and 60 percent of the entire population. The other mtDNA strands found in Europe account for between 0 and 15 percent each — which gives an idea of the dominance of Haplogroup H in this regard.

In Britain, H runs at 42 percent in England, 42.5 percent in Scotland, 43 percent in Wales and 38.5 percent in Ireland. An average for all of Britain (excluding Ireland) is therefore 42.5 percent.

A 2008 study showed that Haplogroup H was present in Europe at least 28,000 ybp and spread across the continent. Similar studies suggest that many of the H subclades, namely H1, H3 and its "sister Haplogroup" V, are representative of a second wave of migration northwest into Europe after the end of the last ice age, about 12,000 ybp.

As a result, H1, H3 and V are the most common subclades in Western Europe. H1 and H3 are found at frequencies of 6.5 percent in England, 3.5 percent in Scotland, and 11 percent in Ireland. It is statistically insignificant in Wales. When the figures for these subclades are added to the main H Haplogroup totals, the final average for Britain (excluding Ireland) rises to around 45 percent.

I

Haplogroup I is another common European haplogroup whose mutations indicate that it first appeared around 40,000 ybp. It was therefore likely to have been one of the very first female lines to appear in Europe and is at least 40,000 years old. It is today found in around 3.5 percent of the English, 5 percent of the Scottish, 6 percent of the Welsh and 3 percent of the Irish. The total for Britain (excluding Ireland) is therefore 4.8 percent.

J

Haplogroup J originated some 50,000 ybp in the Near East and is closely linked to the lineages which spread agriculture into Europe. J runs at 9 percent in England, 14 percent in Scotland, 9.5 percent in Wales and 10 percent in

Ireland. The Scottish figures include a subclade, J1b1, which runs at 4 percent.

Yet another subclade, called J/16231, is regarded as the "Germanic" branch of that haplotype and is found in England at 3 percent and mainland Scotland at 4 percent. It is statistically insignificant in Wales, Cornwall, north and west Scotland, or Ireland.

The average for Britain (excluding Ireland) for haplotype J is therefore of the order of 10.8 percent. This is close to the European average of 11 percent. Certain haplotypes of J2 are distinct to Britain and Scandinavia. This is mostly likely due to a shared Neolithic migratory pattern.

K

Haplogroup K is the most common subclade of Haplogroup U8 and it has an estimated age in Europe of 12,000 ybp. It is particularly common around the Alps and the British Isles. In England, this marker runs at 9.5 percent; in Scotland, 6.5 percent; in Wales, 9.5 percent and in Ireland, 11 percent. The average in Britain (excluding Ireland) is 7.5 percent, compared to a 6 percent average across Europe.

Haplogroup K is also found amongst Jewish people of Ashkenazi ancestry, although its presence in other parts of the world indicates that it is not exclusively a Jewish marker.

The high concentration in Britain is probably linked to a pre-end of the ice age "genetic bottleneck" in Iberia which preceded a migratory wave to the British Isles.

T

Haplogroup T has been shown to derive from Haplogroup JT, which also gave rise to Haplogroup J. The interrelatedness of the two haplogroups is reflected in their origins in the Near East at least 45,000 years ago and their spread into Europe at the end of the last ice age.

As a result, Haplogroup T is widely distributed in Europe. In Britain, it is found at 11 percent in England, 11.5 percent in Scotland, 11 percent in Wales and 12 percent in Ireland. This compares with the 10 percent average found in the rest of Europe and is considered a signature of the settlers who brought large-scale agriculture to Europe.

The origin of Haplogroup T1 appears to be more recent, although these dates are all relative. T1 dates to at least 6,000 ybp. The T2 subclade is an older line and appears to

Section Four: Haplogroups Found in Britain

have been present even earlier.

U

Haplogroup U has been dated at about 55,000 ybp. It is divided up into a number of subclades, only some of which are represented in Europe. Haplogroup U is found at 14 percent in England, 13 percent in Scotland, 10 percent in Wales and 13 percent in Ireland. The average for Britain, excluding Ireland, is therefore 12.3 percent.

Haplogroups U2, U3, and U4 are also found in Britain at relatively low frequencies, ranging from 0 to 2.5 percent at their highest. They are all dated at approximately 25,000 ybp and are linked to the settlement of Europe before the end of the last ice age.

Haplogroup U5 is one of the oldest mtDNA haplotypes found in Europe. Some studies have claimed that it is an astonishing 60,500 years old. About 11 percent of Europeans (and 10 percent of European-Americans) are members of this haplogroup.

In England, U5 runs at 8 percent; in Scotland, at 7 percent; in Wales, at 4.5 percent and in Ireland, at 6 percent, giving an average for Britain (excluding Ireland) of 6.5 percent.

V

Haplogroup V is believed to have originated around the western Mediterranean region, about 15,000 ybp. Studies suggest it originated in Iberia. The closely related populations of the British Isles and Iberia might explain the appearance of this haplogroup in Britain, even though it is proportionally very small. In England, V runs at 3.5 percent; in Scotland, at 3.5 percent; in Wales, at 1.5 percent and in Ireland, at 4 percent, giving an average for Britain (excluding Ireland) of 2.8 percent.

W

Haplogroup W is a line closely associated with the Indo-European group. It is concentrated in Western Europe (and Spain in particular) from where the small British element appears to derive. In England, W runs at 2 percent; in Scotland, at 1 percent; in Wales, it is statistically insignificant, and in Ireland, it runs at 2.5 percent, giving an average for Britain (excluding Ireland) of 1 percent.

Studies indicate that W is derived from the parent

Haplogroup N, which has been dated to 65,000 ybp. W is a mere youngster by comparison, being dated at "only" 25,000 ybp.

The W Haplogroup entered Western Europe at the end of the last ice age, and is now found in Ireland. A subclade is also presumed to have arrived in Britain from Germany.

X

Haplogroup X also originally derived from the N Haplogroup, with further mutations occurring about 25,000 ybp. It accounts for about 2 percent of the European population, and was part of the post ice age repopulation of the continent.

In Britain it is concentrated in the Orkney Islands at 7 percent as the subclade X2, but is far lower elsewhere in the country. The frequency of X2 in England runs at 1.5 percent, in Scotland 1.5 percent (indicating how low it must be in order for the Orkney result to be submerged amongst the other Scottish averages), in Wales 1 percent and in Ireland at 1.5 percent. This gives an average for Britain (excluding Ireland) of around 1 percent.

* Note: In all of the averages, the Republic of Ireland has been excluded despite being referenced.

This is done specifically to illustrate the homogeneity of the United Kingdom, but the reality which becomes clear upon reading the statistics is that the Irish share a huge commonality with the Welsh, the Scottish and the English.

In what might come as a shock to many Scots-Irish, the Scots in fact share far more in common, genetically speaking, with the Irish than they do with the English.

Section Five: *A History of the Populating of Britain*

A review of the genetic evidence leads inevitably to the conclusion that the vast majority of the population of the British Isles have ancestors going back at least 12,000 years, and in some cases, considerably longer than that.

This has important implications for the history of the populating of Britain and equally significant ramifications to support the case for an indigenous population of our isles.

In essence, the vast majority of the British genetic stock is comprised of a wave of settlers who arrived in Britain at the end of the last ice age.

The current scientific thinking is that this wave of settlers was, in fact, a repopulation of Britain after the ice age forced most people south. This train of thought must have some accuracy to it, as the skeletal evidence (reviewed below) would indicate that there were people present in parts of Britain either before or during the ice age (which never fully covered all of Britain's landmass).

In any event, what is beyond question is that the majority of our ancestors came here as hunter-gatherers between 15,000 and 7,500 years ago. This would have been just after the last ice sheets, which ran in a line across central England, melted away, and before the rising sea waters finally cut the land off from continental Europe.

No Population Replacement since End of Last Ice Age

The genetic evidence shows clearly that this settlement of Britain which followed the ice age laid the basis for the modern European British population and that all subsequent invasions or migrations occurred on a relatively small scale.

More importantly, none of these invasions ever replaced the original population. Previously, historians subscribed to this "mass replacement" theory, which in turn gave rise to the now-often repeated "nation of immigrants" propaganda line.

The "nation of immigrants" theory has proven to be completely false. DNA has allowed the accurate quantification of each invasion and settlement.

The genetic evidence shows, for example, that the division between the west and east of England did not result from the "Anglo-Saxon invasion" but rather from a much older

Four Flags: The Indigenous People of Britain

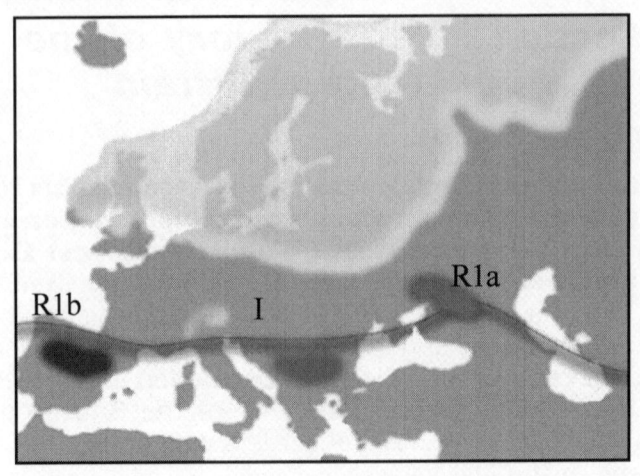

Europe 18,000 Years Before Present (YBP). The presence of the three main Y-Chromosome haplogroups is marked, as are the extent of the glaciers from the last ice age. The line running across the map from Spain to the Caspian Sea is the "tree line," north of which only grasslands were able to survive the cold. This map does not show Britain joined to the landmass of continental Europe, as it would have been. Britain and Ireland only separated from the Continent about 6500 YBP.

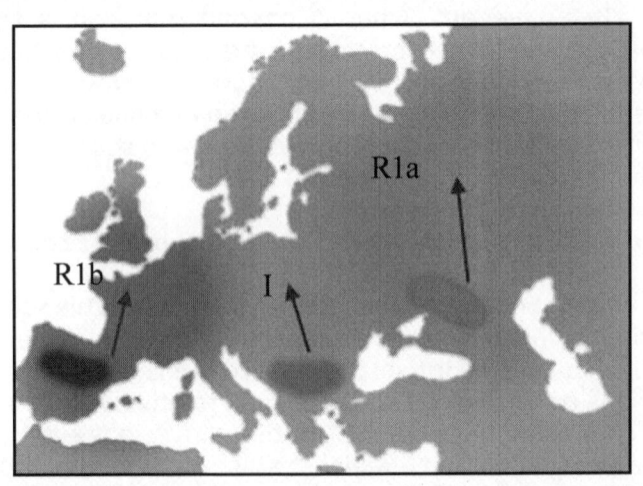

Europe 12,000 YBP showing how the haplogroups R1b, I and R1a spread northwards following the final end of the last ice age. The long period for which the groups were halted on their migration northwards helped create the mutations which have allowed their individual identification. This is why R1b is common in the far west of Europe (Britain included); I is common in central Europe and Scandinavia; and R1a is common in Eastern Europe. These three haplogroups account for at least 80 percent of Europe's native population and all ultimately have a common root.

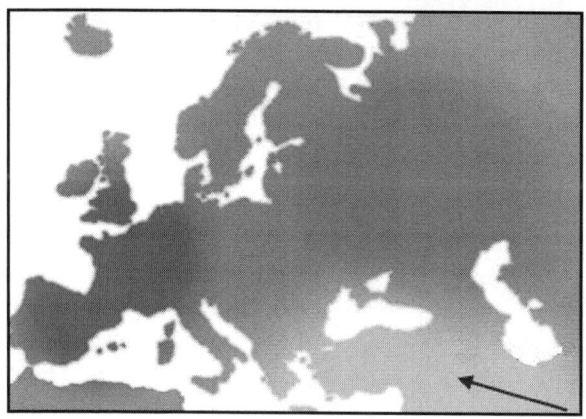

Section Five: A History of the Populating of Britain

Europe circa 8000 YBP, showing the route of the Neolithic era migrations into Europe from the Middle East. The main haplogroups identified in this movement were E3b, F, J2 and G2. These migrations are commonly associated with the spread of organised agriculture into Europe.

— by thousands and thousands of years — origin with two main routes of genetic flow.

The First Wave: The "R1b" Settlers

The first major settlement of Britain originated from western Europe by the European people who carried the R1b Haplogroup.

This group is today still the dominant Y-Chromosome European haplogroup found in Iberia and the British Isles, which has led some to claim that the British people are "Iberians" or "Basques."

This is, of course, a simplification. What actually happened was that the peoples who settled Iberia also settled Britain, and once in their respective territories, were subjected to other genetic and cultural influences which created the modern European nations of Britain, Ireland, Spain and Portugal. Nonetheless, it is true that the R1b Y-Chromosome haplotype is found in greater frequencies in those nations than anywhere else in Europe, allowing geneticists to cluster them together when creating DNA maps of Europe.

Upper Palaeolithic Settlement

It is still a matter of conjecture if the population of Northwest Europe was retreating before the ice sheets or if they were advancing as the glaciers melted.

Four Flags: The Indigenous People of Britain

Nonetheless, the first human settlers in Britain arrived during the Upper Palaeolithic period around 32,000 YBP — right in the middle of the last ice age which ran from approximately 70,000 YBP to 12,000 YBP. This period is known as the time of the Aurignacian culture.

The Red Lady of Paviland

The most famous example of an Upper Palaeolithic burial site dating from this period is in South Wales. The skeleton recovered at that site is known as the "Red Lady of Paviland."

The site also produced numerous artefacts dating from the Upper Palaeolithic period, including a mammoth skull. The skeleton, incorrectly identified as a female by its discoverer, was covered in red ochre (commonly used in burials in ancient Europe) and was called the "Red Lady of Paviland" as a result.

The "Red Lady of Paviland" skeleton exhibition in the National Museum in Cardiff. The Upper Palaeolithic burial has been dated to 26,000 YBP.

The skeleton has been accurately dated to 26,000 YBP and is most likely a fine example of Cro-Magnon European man. Other excavations at the Paviland burial site produced flint, ivory and bone artefacts going back to around 35,000 YBP.

DNA research in Europe has found that the dominant haplogroup amongst Cro-Magnons was the "N" type which is the basis for almost all modern European haplotypes, and the R1 group in particular.

Molecular biologist Bryan Sykes has shown that the "Red Lady" has a DNA sequence which matches the R1 lineage. It is not beyond the realms of possibility, therefore, that the Paviland skeleton represents one of the oldest inhabitant groups in all Britain, a record which would then stretch back deep into the last ice age.

Section Five: A History of the Populating of Britain

Creswell Crags and Gough's Cave

Another Upper Palaeolithic site which shows that the earliest British inhabitants were present on this island nation tens of thousands of years ago, has been found at the Creswell Crags, a gorge in Derbyshire, in the East Midlands. There, several caves have produced archaeological evidence of modern human habitation dating at between 40,000 and 10,000 YBP.

The relatively northern position of the Cresswell site is a further indicator of a more widespread Upper Palaeolithic presence in Britain.

The region would only have just been free of the retreating glaciers, and for it to have been inhabited at that early stage must imply a relatively large population further south.

The Gough's Cave site in Somerset has been dated at 14,000 YBP, putting it at the very end of the Upper Palaeolithic period.

Mesolithic Settlement

Around 12,000 YBP, the ice age finally ended, giving rise to what is known as the Mesolithic period. Some 9,500 years ago, rising temperatures caused sea levels to rise as the glaciers melted. By 6000 BC, Britain and Ireland had been cut off from continental Europe and each other by the rising waters — and by this time the major repopulation of the British Isles had been completed.

Evidence of human habitation in Britain during this time period extends to the north of Scotland, the Mendips in Somerset, Star Carr in Yorkshire, Oronsay in the Hebrides, Howick in Northumberland (where the foundations of a large circular house dating 8500 YBP were found), and Deepcar in Sheffield.

The increasing population density led to the development of large-scale agriculture as well.

Cheddar Man

The most prominent example of an early Briton from this period is the famous Cheddar Man, found in the Cheddar Gorge, in Somerset. Dated at around 8000 YBP, DNA analysis on one of this skeleton's teeth identified his mitochondrial DNA as being from Haplogroup U5, one of the types still found in Britain today.

Four Flags: The Indigenous People of Britain

In 1996, DNA samples were taken from the living residents of Cheddar Village near the gorge by molecular scientist Bryan Sykes. A comparison with the DNA extracted from Cheddar Man produced two exact matches and one more match with a single mutation between the samples.

The results proved a continuous lineage of people in that part of Britain going back nearly 9,000 years.

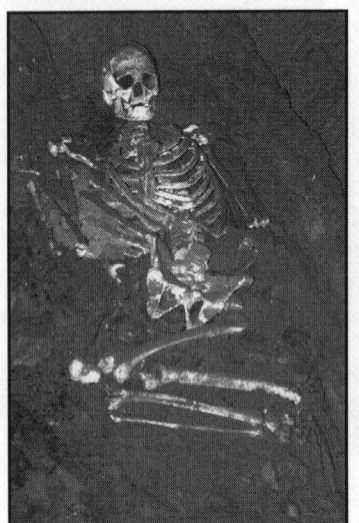

Cheddar Man, as he was found in the Cheddar Gorge, Mendip, Somerset. (The skeleton is in a local museum, and this display is a reconstruction in the cave on the spot where he was found.) DNA tests have shown this 8000 YBP man had direct descendants still living in the village of Cheddar in 1996. This is remarkable evidence of continuous settlement for thousands of years.

Neolithic Settlement

The Neolithic period — dated at between 6000 and 4000 YBP, was marked by the introduction of large-scale farming industries in Britain. The introduction of these farming methods has traditionally been associated with the arrival of the "Indo-European" culture and language bearing peoples from the Middle East.

It was during the Neolithic period that the great hill forts, earthen walls, burial place barrows and great wood and stone henges were built. The most famous of these is, of course, Stonehenge, but there are a great number of similar sites to be found all over all over England, Wales, Scotland and Ireland. The Neolithic era also saw the introduction of ironworking, which replaced bronze as the metal of choice, bringing an end to the Bronze Age.

The Stonehenge Archer

Possibly the most famous examples from this time period are a group of skeletons found in Wiltshire. The first of these is known as the "Stonehenge Archer," the name given to the skeleton of a Bronze Age man discovered in 1978, buried in an outer ditch at Stonehenge in Wiltshire. The "archer" name was given to it because of the stone wrist-guard and flint arrowheads found in the grave.

Later forensic examination of the skeleton indicated that the man was local to the area, while radiocarbon dating found that he died around 4300 YBP.

The Amesbury Archer

The second skeleton, discovered in 2002, was found in Amesbury, only a few miles from Stonehenge. Known as the Amesbury Archer (also because of the wrist guard and arrowheads found with him), this skeleton has also been dated from approximately 4300 YBP. Gold discovered with the body has been dated to 4470 YBP, making it the oldest gold artefacts yet discovered in Britain.

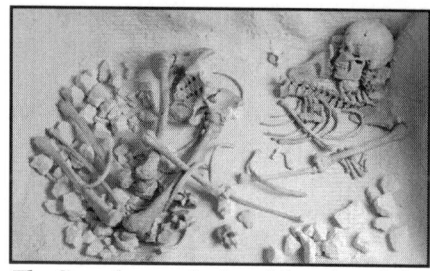

The Stonehenge Archer (above) and the Amesbury Archer (below). Two Neolithic era skeletons discovered in Wiltshire. DNA analysis on the Amesbury Archer has shown that he originated in the Alps. Both on display at the Salisbury Museum.

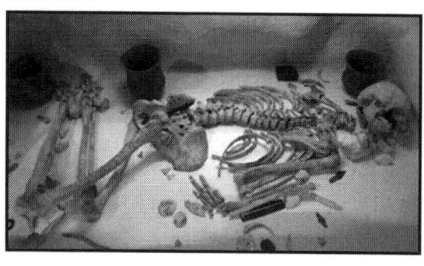

The Amesbury Archer provides genetic evidence of Celtic-bearing limited immigration from Europe during the Neolithic period. Detailed DNA analysis using oxygen isotopes in his tooth enamel showed that he was originally from the Alps region, probably Switzerland, Austria or Germany.

In addition, the copper knives found with the Amesbury Archer came from Spain and France.

The Boscombe Bowmen

In 2003, a third set of skeletons, known as the Boscombe Bowmen, were discovered in communal graves on Boscombe Down, also near Stonehenge.

Seven skeletons were found at this site. Lead isotope analysis of the teeth from some of the remains showed that they also date from around 4300 YBP. The analysis also showed that the individuals were born in Wales or the Lake District of England's northwest. Their place of origin indicates that they were involved with the building of Stonehenge, as the Sarsen

Circle at that monument consists of stones which were transported to Wiltshire from Wales.

The Indo-European and "Celtic" Influence

As evidenced by the Amesbury Archer, the DNA evidence indicates that there was an input from central Europe into Britain. The numbers involved do not appear to be as large as many historical accounts have claimed.

Mitochondrial DNA from all over Europe indicates that 80 percent of the population in the female line comes from settlements into Europe prior to the Neolithic Age. Less than 20 percent are descended from the later migrants with whom the agricultural revolution is traditionally associated, and in Britain, this figure drops to 11 percent.

This would also have been the time of the settlement of the small "Celtic" culture bearing peoples in Europe, although there is still great debate as to how widespread this actually was.

In any event, the closeness of the DNA types between these subclades and the length of time they have been in Europe — and Britain — makes any attempts to differentiate between them of academic interest only. The reality is that the native peoples of Europe show a huge degree of genetic similarity, and have forbearers going back thousands, and even tens of thousands of years, in their ancestral homelands.

The R1b migrations did not carry with them the "Celtic" culture or language. These Celtic languages and culture bearers arrived during the Neolithic period, several thousand years after the R1b settlement.

Those areas which have culturally become "Celtic" heartlands (Ireland, Wales and Scotland) actually had less input from the European continent "Celtic" peoples than England.

The Celtic culture was, the DNA evidence shows, carried into western Europe by small bands of agriculturalists along the north Mediterranean to Italy, France, Spain and Britain.

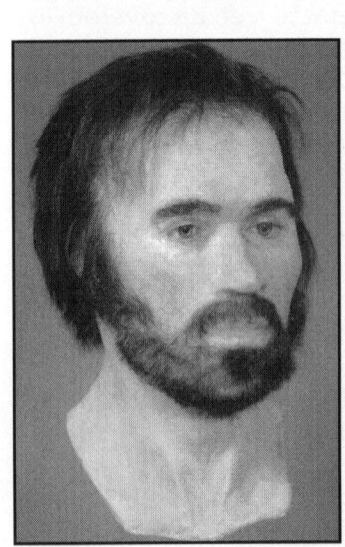

A reconstruction of the head of Lindow Man, the Iron Age (100 AD) body found in a Cheshire bog in 1984.

Section Five: A History of the Populating of Britain

Even this process of "Johnny-Come-Lately" settlement was completed some 5,700 years ago, easily qualifying this small group of Celtic culture bearers as indigenous by any stretch of the imagination.

In western England, Wales and Scotland the proportion of northwestern European input drops dramatically. For example, the R1b type is found at its "lowest" in Fakenham, Norfolk, on the east coast — where it still comprises 59 percent of the local total.

In Llangefni, North Wales, the R1b type reaches its highest percentage (96 percent) in Britain. This haplotype is found at its highest rate (93 percent) in Ireland around Castlerea.

The Roman Invasion

The next event of significance in Britain's settlement was the Roman invasion and conquest. As the might of Rome grew on the Continent, small groups of people known as the Belgae (from modern day France and Belgium) fled across the English Channel from the victorious Romans, settling around Portsmouth and Winchester. Their numbers were, however, comparatively insignificant and their genetic footprint is so close to the British as to be invisible in terms of DNA analysis.

According to Roman records, their invasion force consisted of around 40,000 regular troops and auxiliaries. The majority of this force was withdrawn after the fighting ended, and the Romans kept around 16,000 soldiers in the various legions stationed around the country.

Compared to the size of the British population, the Roman numbers were tiny. Estimates of the total number of native inhabitants around the year 0 AD are put at 1 million, rising to nearly 2 million by 200 AD.

From this, the few tens of thousands of Roman occupation forces (which came from various places in the Roman Empire), it can be seen that the Roman genetic influence would have been minimal, and limited to a very few areas of concentrated settlements.

The Post-Roman Invasions 400-700 AD

The withdrawal of the last Roman legions in 410 AD set the scene for a number of invasions from the European continent. The Angles, Saxons, Jutes, Frisians and Franks, all

Four Flags: The Indigenous People of Britain

Germanic peoples from western and central Europe, settled in Britain in varying numbers.

It has traditionally been thought that the Anglo-Saxons had a major impact upon the population make-up of Britain. However, their numbers appear to have been only in the thousands, and their genetic impact upon the British population bears this out.

The genetic evidence shows that the "Anglo-Saxon race" in England does not exist in any significant form, which is another bitter pill for many.

The idea of an all-powerful "Anglo-Saxon race" became common in Victorian times, possibly as a self-feeding justification for the enormous success of the British Empire which reached its most dizzying heights at that time.

The DNA evidence however shows that the influence of the Anglo-Saxon invasion from western Germany was actually quite minor and that there is no basis for claiming that group as a founding gene pool in Britain. The impact of the Anglo-Saxon and German "settlement" seems to have been more on a cultural level rather than causing any large population displacement.

The Viking Invasions 789–1104 AD

The first recorded Viking attack on Britain took place in 789. Thereafter followed a period of extended Viking (Danes and other Scandinavians) settlement in the north of Britain, centred around York. As a result, Viking genes are most commonly found in East Anglia, York, northeast Scotland and the Orkney Islands. Viking genes are marked by the R1a marker, which is not surprisingly found at its highest in York.

The Viking settlements sparked off a series of conflicts and by 886 AD, King Alfred the Great had nearly defeated the invasion. As a concession, he allowed the Vikings to settle in eastern England around the kingdoms of York and East Anglia. This was the area which became known as the Danelaw.

The Danelaw was, however, wrested back by the Britons in a series of conflicts which raged from 901–937 AD, and by 954 AD, Eric Bloodaxe, the last Viking king of Jorvik (York), was expelled.

The Vikings had in the interim also settled in Ireland. From there they launched attacks on the west coast of Britain, sweeping up and down the Welsh coast, the Merseyside and reaching as far north as the Hebrides in Scotland.

Section Five: A History of the Populating of Britain

A reconstruction of a Viking settlement in York, as on display at the Jorvik Viking centre in that city. The Viking gene is most common on the eastern side of Britain, although strong traces have been identified in the Merseyside area which is related to Viking conquests from Ireland.

A 2008 study conducted by scientists from the Universities of Nottingham, Leicester and University College London, revealed that in certain areas of the northwest of England, up to 50 percent of the male population carries Norse origin genes — the same as modern Orkney. This has been directly linked to the Viking incursions from Ireland, but, as on the east coast of England, is limited to certain areas only.

The actual numbers of Vikings who settled in the British Isles has always been a point of dispute. Contemporary descriptions of Viking raiding parties never list more than a few dozen attackers (the contents of a handful of Viking boats — for example, the most famous Viking invaders, Hengist and Horsa, are described as having come over in three ships), but logic dictates that this number must have increased after the establishment of Viking settlements.

Even so, the number of Viking settlers could not have numbered more than a few thousand in total, and expressed as a percentage of the total population of the British Isles, was comparatively small, even after the Danish King Canute captured the English crown in 1016. Not surprisingly, the DNA evidence has confirmed these relatively small numbers and once averaged out, the amount of "Viking blood" amongst the British population is around 5 percent.

The Viking influence in Britain was therefore relatively small and limited to the ruling elite. Even this process was not particularly long-lasting.

For example, Canute married Emma, the widow of the English king deposed by the Danish invasion — but their son, Harthacnut, was succeeded by Edward II (the Confessor), who was the son of Emma by her first husband. Within a generation, the Danish influence on the royal line had been removed.

When Edward died without children, Emma's great-nephew, Duke William of Normandy, laid claim to the English throne. William famously invaded Britain in 1066 and brought a final end to the Viking claims on England although they persisted in Scotland until 1104 when the last of the Viking settlements were dissipated in the western isles.

The Norman Conquest

The invasion of Britain in 1066 by William the Conqueror and the Normans has gained almost mythical status in British history. Certainly it had a cultural impact upon Britain, but, as the DNA evidence now shows, it hardly impacted upon the population of Britain.

Records show that William's army was only about 7,000 strong at the famous Battle of Hastings, a time when his invasion force would in all likelihood have been at its strongest.

Furthermore, once he was secure in his new dominion, he paid off this largely mercenary army in 1070 and nearly all of them returned to their homes in France.

It is therefore likely that the Norman invasion did not contain more than a few thousand men in total, at a time when the total population of Britain was estimated at over three million. As a result, the genetic impact of the Norman invasion is almost undetectable.

Normans Were Last Incursion

The tiny Norman "invasion" (which was actually just a replacement of the royal line, as the figures show) was the last time Britain was subjected to a serious invasion — until large-scale Third World immigration into Britain was started after World War II.

Section Five: A History of the Populating of Britain

The 1066 Norman invasion fleet (Bayeaux Tapestry). Although of great historical significance, the Norman invasion left no genetic impact on Britain due to their tiny numbers.

Between the Normans and the Third World immigration invasion of the late twentieth century, a number of minor other settlements took place, which have all been inconsequential in numerical and DNA terms. These migrations have included Jews and small numbers of continental Europeans, all worthy of a brief overview.

When Edward I expelled the Jews from Britain in 1290, the total numbers involved were only 5,000, compared to the total population of nearly 4 million.

By 1815, the Jewish population had risen to around 25,000. Their numbers were boosted by a migration from Eastern Europe and Russia prior to World War I. This figure was topped up by a further migration from Germany and Europe prior to World War II, which resulted in a Jewish population today of some 300,000. Many of these have been completely assimilated, leaving little distinguishable imprint.

A small migration of people from Belgium, the Netherlands, Luxembourg and parts of northern France and Germany entered Britain between the fourteenth and sixteenth centuries, fleeing conflict and religious persecution on the Continent. Their total numbers were put at 16,000 in 1440, another tiny figure which had no major genetic impact on the British population.

From 1680 to 1720, French Huguenots, fleeing Catholic persecution in France, settled in Britain. Their figures never reached more than 50,000 over the four decades of immigration, also a tiny amount when compared to the estimated 6 million strong population of Britain in the year 1700.

Other immigrations from across Europe up to the Second World War included a handful of Germans and Italians (the 1871 census reported 32,823 Germans and 5,063 Italians in England and Wales, with an even smaller number in Scotland).

African Slaves and Their Expulsion

The only other historic migration of note prior to World War II resulted from Britain's involvement in the trans-Atlantic slave trade. Most Africans brought to Britain (via the slave trading ports of Bristol and Liverpool) were immediately shipped on to the New World, but a few remained in Britain as servants.

It is estimated that some 20,000 were present in Britain in 1596 and 1601 when Queen Elizabeth I issued her famous expulsion orders of the "divers blackmoores brought into this realme, of which kinde of people there are allready here to manie."

The 1601 proclamation added that Queen Elizabeth was "highly discontented to understand the great numbers of negars and Blackamoores which are crept into this realm ... who are fostered and relieved here to the great annoyance of her own liege people ... should be with all speed avoided and discharged out of this Her Majesty's dominions."

This expulsion reduced the number of Africans in Britain to a handful — estimated at no more than one or two thousand at most. Once again, this would have had no significant impact upon the make-up of the population of Britain.

Up to 80 Percent of Population from a Single Source

If the interrelatedness of the various R1b subclades and the R1a Haplotype are taken into account, then it becomes possible to say that at least 80 or more percent of Britain's population derives from a single source. Even the individual non-R1b inputs do not make up more than five percent each.

This effectively "kills" not only the "nation of immigrants" story, but some other cherished ideas about the history of the population of Britain, most notably the "Celtic" and "Anglo-Saxon" origins — and therefore the long-standing "division" between "Celtic" Ireland and mainland Britain.

Section Five: A History of the Populating of Britain

The Interrelatedness of the Irish, Welsh, Scottish and Most of England

All of the above leads to the undeniable conclusion that the Irish have far more in common with the mainland British population than what many on both sides of that traditional divide might want to be the case.

Genetically speaking, the population of Ireland, Wales, Scotland and western England are indistinguishable. Even in eastern England, an outright majority of the population are equally indistinguishable from the Irish. It is a sobering perspective on history.

Conclusion

The historical record therefore matches the DNA evidence closely. Both show that the vast majority of the indigenous population of the British Isles have been resident there for many thousands of years.

Furthermore, the DNA evidence confirms that prior to the post-World War II Third World wave of immigration, the small and limited numbers of European immigrants into Britain were of almost identical genetic stock and as such hardly had any impact upon the population.

Section Six: *The Rights of the Indigenous People of Britain*

THE existence of an indigenous people in the British Isles is conclusively confirmed by the historical and genetic record. Nearly 80 percent of indigenous British people are descendants of Neolithic era or earlier settlers, with some going back into Upper Palaeolithic times — up to 26,000 or more years ago.

Even many of the remaining 20 percent have been in Britain since the late Neolithic era, or at the very latest (the Viking and Danish migrations) since 700 or 800 AD, making them resident here for at least 1300 years.

How does this compare with other peoples around the world who are already considered indigenous?

The Māori of New Zealand

The Māori people are fully recognised by all international bodies, including the United Nations, as being the indigenous people of New Zealand.

They have representation on the United Nations Permanent Forum on Indigenous Issues and have fully qualified under all the admission requirements.

The Māori have their own language, culture and tradition, and their lands are protected by law from outside invasion. The government of New Zealand has formally negotiated with Māori to "provide redress for breaches by the Crown" of land guarantees made in earlier treaties between the European settlers and the indigenous people.

In particular, the New Zealand authorities had, by 2006, given millions in settlement payments to the Māori, most of it in land deals. In one settlement, signed in June

A classic tourist image of a Māori from New Zealand. Although officially recognised as an indigenous people by all international organisations, they have only been in New Zealand for around 730 years — literally thousands of years after the British Isles were settled.

Section Six: *The Rights of the Indigenous People of Britain*

2008, nine huge areas of land were formally handed over to exclusive Māori control.

Their special status is so entrenched that there are seven designated Māori-only seats in the parliament of New Zealand.

How long have the Māori people been in New Zealand? The answer is: about 730 years.

The first Māori settlement of New Zealand has been accurately dated as having occurred around the year 1280 AD. The Māori arrived in southwestern Polynesia in several waves some time before 1300, with their mtDNA analysis suggesting an origin in Taiwan some 5,200 years ago.

In other words, the Māori people have been in New Zealand for less time than the "youngest" inhabitant group of the British Isles, yet still firmly qualify for indigenous status under all international treaties and conventions.

The Aborigines of Australia

The indigenous people of Australia are the Aboriginal people and the Torres Island Straits people. Both have representation on the UN Permanent Forum on Indigenous Issues and are in fact genetically distinguishable from one another.

There are about 500 different Aboriginal clans in Australia, each with their own claim to territory and, in many cases, entire towns.

They receive vast amounts of taxpayer subsidies, and two laws have been enacted to specifically cater for their needs: the Aboriginal Lands Trust Act 1966, and the Aboriginal Heritage Act, 1988.

The Australian government also has an "Aboriginal Affairs and Reconciliation Division" and a "Department of Families, Community Services and Indigenous Affairs" devoted to serving the interests of the Aboriginal people.

The Torres Strait Islands are in Queensland, and their inhabitants are genetically linked to the Melanesian peoples of Papua New Guinea. They, too, have all manner of special status and subsidies catering specifically to their needs — and territories set aside for their use.

How long have the Aborigines been in Australia?

The oldest existing skeleton which has been linked to the Aboriginal people was found near Mungo Lake, New South Wales, and has been dated as 40,000 years old.

There is still dispute in scientific circles as to when exactly the main body of Aborigines entered Australia, but it is

A group of Australian Aborigines perform a ritual dance. The earliest date of human habitation in Australia is estimated to be between 40,000 and 30,000 YBP. This compares with the oldest evidence of human habitation in Britain, at Creswell Crags in Derbyshire, also dated at around 40,000 YBP.

accepted that the remains found at Mungo Lake ("Mungo Man") mark out the very earliest date at which the Aboriginal people first entered Australia.

However, this date is unlikely to be accurate because the Aboriginal population numbers at the time of the first permanent European settlement were so tiny — estimated at between 318,000 and 750,000. If the Aborigines had been in Australia for 40,000 years, their numbers would have had to been considerably higher than three quarters of a million.

Hence a much more recent date for the first Aboriginal settlement is likely, but unproven. In any event even taking the Aboriginal presence to be 30,000 years old, this is still only (in relative terms) marginally older than the 26,000-year old "Red Lady of Paviland" skeleton found in Wales.

In addition, evidence of human habitation at the Creswell Crags in Derbyshire has also been dated to about 40,000 YBP.

Hence, even by using Australian Aborigines as a basis of measurement, the British people still qualify as an indigenous people.

The People of Tibet

The Tibetan people are indigenous to Tibet and are one of the favourite cause célèbres amongst many liberals in Europe who object to the Han Chinese immigration into that autonomous region.

The reality of the Chinese settlement of Tibet — which will result in the swamping of the Tibetan people and culture – is, however, a matter of serious concern as it will lead to the extinction of the Tibetans as a distinct ethnic group and culture.

The Tibetans are marked by a large preponderance of Haplogroup D-M174 which makes them quite distinct from the majority of their neighbours. The DNA shows, however, that

Section Six: *The Rights of the Indigenous People of Britain*

the ancestors of the Tibetans entered Tibet some 3000 YBP.

This means that the Tibetan people — who are (correctly) the subject of much international uproar over the possibility that they might lose their indigenous status before a wave of Chinese immigration — are younger than almost all of the inhabitants of the British Isles, by thousands and thousands of years.

The people of Tibet are accepted as an indigenous nation under threat from mass Han Chinese immigration. DNA evidence has shown that the Tibetans entered that region about 3000 YBP. This is several thousand years younger than the majority of the population

The Indians of North America

The Indians of North America prefer to be called Indians instead of "Native Americans" but steadfastly stick to their claim of being the indigenous peoples of that continent. The Indians, genetically linked to Asia, were apparently part of a population movement from Western Asia across the Bering Strait (which, according to the migration theory, was a landmass at the time) and from there populated the Americas in waves going south.

The American Indians had an unfortunate history after 1492, and were steadily driven west across North America as the European settlements advanced.

Largely because of this process, the American government finally granted the Indians special status as an indigenous people so that today there are no less than 310 Indian reservations in America, which are specifically reserved for Indians and no-one else.

The American government also has a dedicated Bureau of Indian Affairs which has no other purpose but to look to the interests of the Indian population. The Indians also have their own recognised system of Chiefdoms, protection of their language and culture, and receive massive subsidies from the taxpayer in one form or another.

In addition, they have the right in their reservations to make local laws and rules specific to themselves, an arrangement which is possibly best known for the creation of casinos on Indian lands. The American Indians are possibly one of the most "commercialised" of all the officially recognised

Four Flags: The Indigenous People of Britain

A photograph of the famous nineteenth century Apache chief Geronimo who fought Mexican and white American expansion into his lands until his capture in 1905. The American Indian people are formally recognised as "Native Americans" and have entire government departments (and even a national museum in Washington DC) dedicated to them. The first formally recognised American Indian culture is known as Clovis, dated at around 9000 YBP. All the evidence indicates that the first Indians penetrated North America after 12,000 YBP — exactly the same time that the first major repopulation of the British Isles occurred.

indigenous peoples of the world, and the Indian warrior, his headdress and bow and arrow have entered the world of literature and art like few other peoples have. They are, of course, important players in the United Nations Permanent Forum on Indigenous Issues.

So how long have the American Indians been in North America?

Scientists and historians have, through a process of elimination and genetics, put the entry date of the Indians into North America at around 12,000 YBP. Other waves would have followed at a later date, and the "Clovis culture" which marks the first important Indian culture has been dated at around 9000 YBP.

In other words, the officially acknowledged and accepted indigenous people of North America have been on that continent for almost the exact same length of time as the vast majority of the inhabitants of the British Isles.

The Amazon Indians and Indigenous Peoples of South America

There are a vast number of tribes and indigenous peoples in South America, concentrated in Brazil, Columbia, Ecuador, Peru, Venezuela and Guyana.

Those living in the Amazon rain forests have traditionally caught the public's attention. Their completely correct and justifiable pleas for protection against encroaching industrialisation, forest logging and the resultant destruction

Section Six: *The Rights of the Indigenous People of Britain*

A recent photograph of a group of Amazonian Indians. They and other native peoples of South America have official indigenous status and are afforded protection by and representation on the United Nations Permanent Forum for Indigenous Affairs. Archaeological and DNA evidence shows that the earliest human habitation in South America occurred around 6000 YBP and the earliest identifiable culture about 2000 YBP. The Amazonian Indians are also thousands of years younger than the population of Britain.

of their way of life have also become popular and trendy issues to support.

A few of the more prominent tribes (by no means a comprehensive list) include the Akuntsu, Awá, Enawene Nawe, Guarani, Indians of Raposa–Serra do Sol and the Yanomami, all found in Brazil along with other "Brazilian Indians"; the Arhuaco and Nukak in Colombia; the Ayoreo and Enxet in Paraguay; the so-called "Uncontacted Indians of Peru"; and the Wichí of Argentina. All of these people (except for the "uncontacted" ones, for obvious reasons) are feted the world over as indigenous peoples in danger of extinction. They also have representation on the United Nations Permanent Forum on Indigenous Issues.

So how long have the indigenous people of South America been present in their territories which are now under threat?

The first evidence for the existence of organised human habitation in South America dates back to 6500 YBP, when food was first cultivated in the Amazon Basin. The earliest pottery finds have been dated at 2000 YBP, while the famous Incas (to be conquered by the Spanish during the age of the Conquistadors) established their Kingdom of Cuzco around 1200 AD, or about 800 years ago.

Once again, the indigenous people of South America and the Amazonian rain forest, who are internationally acknowledged as indigenous peoples, are many thousands of years younger than the vast majority of the inhabitants of the British Isles.

The Rights of Indigenous People

As outlined in the second section of this work, section 8 of the United Nations Declaration on the Rights of Indigenous Peoples is very clear on the rights of native peoples. It states that
"1. Indigenous peoples and individuals have the right not to be subjected to forced assimilation or destruction of their culture."

As the historical and genetic record in Britain and elsewhere in the world conclusively shows, the rights of the indigenous people of the British Isles are being grossly violated through mass immigration which is directly leading to the forced assimilation and destruction of their culture.

In addition, the rights of the native people of Britain, as defined in section 2 of the UN Declaration, are also being grossly violated on the same grounds. These rights are:
"2. States shall provide effective mechanisms for prevention of, and redress for:
(a) Any action which has the aim or effect of depriving them of their integrity as distinct peoples, or of their cultural values or ethnic identities;
(b) Any action which has the aim or effect of dispossessing them of their lands, territories or resources;
(c) Any form of forced population transfer which has the aim or effect of violating or undermining any of their rights;
(d) Any form of forced assimilation or integration;
(e) Any form of propaganda designed to promote or incite racial or ethnic discrimination directed against them."

Mass immigration is subjecting the British people to the loss of their integrity as distinct peoples. Demographic projections show that, unless halted and reversed, current immigration levels will see the indigenous people of Britain reduced to minority status within the next 40 years.

Furthermore, the creation of a state-sponsored "race police" network under the guise of the "Equality and Human Rights Commission" has led to the systematic persecution of indigenous rights activists on the spurious allegations of "racism" while the same exacting standards are not applied to the immigrant population.

In this way, for example, organisations set up to promote the interests of the indigenous population are subjected to vigorous legal action over their membership criteria, while immigrant organisations are free to organise freely on ethnic and racial lines.

Section Six: *The Rights of the Indigenous People of Britain*

The British People are Indigenous

This work has conclusively shown the following:
- The historical record shows that the majority of inhabitants of the British Isles have roots going back to the end of the last ice age, at least 12,000 YBP and in many cases long before that;

- The genetic evidence fully supports the historical record and proves the liberal allegation that Britain is a "nation of immigrants" to be a disgraceful lie;

- Every other people who already have indigenous status on all continents around the globe are either "younger" or of similar age to the indigenous population of Britain.

- In many cases, where the length of continual occupation of territory by indigenous peoples are compared, the British people have been present in their lands far longer than others officially recognised as indigenous;

- The rights of indigenous peoples not to be subjected to forced assimilation and the destruction of their culture, heritage and territory, applies therefore equally to the native people of the British Isles as it does to any other people or nation on earth.

The British Isles are, therefore, rightfully, legally and morally the possession of the Scots, Irish, Welsh and English.

This land belongs to the people of the four flags, and no others. They can now proceed to defend their territorial integrity, heritage, culture, identity and nationhood safe in the knowledge that the rights which they claim for themselves, are identical to those granted to every other indigenous people on earth.

Bibliography

Journals

Alonso S, et al. "The place of the Basques in the European Y-chromosome diversity landscape" *European Journal of Human Genetics,* 2005 Dec; 13(12):1293-302.
Balaresque et al., "A Predominantly Neolithic Origin for European Paternal Lineages", *PLoS Biol.*, 2010 January; 8(1): e1000285. Published online 2010 January 19.
Bird, Steven. "Haplogroup E3b1a2 as a Possible Indicator of Settlement in Roman Britain by Soldiers of Balkan Origin," *Journal of Genetic Genealogy,* 2007 Vol. 3 No. 2
Bowden GR, et al. "Excavating past population structures by surname-based sampling: the genetic legacy of the Vikings in northwest England," *Molecular Biology and Evolution,* 2008 Feb; 25(2):301–9.
Caramelli D, et al., "A 28,000 Years Old Cro-Magnon mtDNA Sequence Differs from All Potentially Contaminating Modern Sequences," *PLoS ONE* 3(7): e2700. Doi:10.1371/ournal.pone 0002700, 2008
Cristian Capelli et al., "A Y Chromosome Census of the British Isles, *Current Biology,* Volume 13, Issue 11, Pages 979–984 (2003).
Cruciani et al., Tracing Past Human Male Movements in Northern/Eastern Africa and Western Eurasia: New Clues from Y-Chromosomal Haplogroups E-M78 and J-M12, *Molecular Biology and Evolution,* 2007 24(6):1300–1311; doi:10.1093
Dupanloup et al., "Estimating the Impact of Prehistoric Admixture on the Genome of Europeans," *Molecular Biology and Evolution,* 21(7):1361-1372. 2004
Helgason, et al. "Estimating Scandinavian and Gaelic Ancestry in the Male Settlers of Iceland," *American Journal of Human Genetics,* 2000 Sep; 67(3):697–717).
Hill, E et al., Y-chromosome variation and Irish origins, *Nature,* Vol 404, 2002.
Jacobi, R.M. and Higham, T.F.G., The 'Red Lady' ages gracefully: New Ultrafiltration AMS determinations from Paviland," *Journal of Human Evolution* Volume 55, Issue 5, November 2008, Pages 898–907
McEvoy, B et al., The Longue Durée of Genetic Ancestry: Multiple Genetic Marker Systems and Celtic Origins on the Atlantic Facade of Europe *American Journal of Human Genetics,* 75:693–702, 2004.

Bibliography

Roewer, L, et al. "Signature of recent historical events in the European Y-chromosomal STR haplotype distribution," *Human Genetics,* 2005 Mar; 116(4):279–91).

Rosser, Zoe et al., "Y-chromosomal diversity in Europe is clinal and influenced primarily by geography," *American Journal of Human Genetics,* 2000 December; 67(6): 1526–1543.

Santos Alonso et al., "The place of the Basques in the European Y-chromosome diversity landscape," *European Journal of Human Genetics,* (2005) 13, 1293–1302. doi:10.1038/sj.ejhg.5201482.

Stephen Oppenheimer, "Myths of British Ancestry," *Prospect,* October 2006, issue 127.

Weale M, et al. "Y Chromosome Evidence for Anglo-Saxon Mass Migration" *Molecular Biology and Evolution,* 2002 Jul; 19(7):1008–21).

Wilson JF, et al. "Genetic evidence for different male and female roles during cultural transitions in the British Isles," Proceedings of the National Academy of Sciences of the United States of America, 2001 Apr 24; 98(9):4830–2).

Books

B. Arredi et al., *Anthropological Genetics: Theory, Methods and Applications.* Cambridge, UK: Cambridge University Press. p. 394.

Cavalli-Sforza, L.L. *Genes, People and Languages.* London: Penguin, 2001.

Kemp, A. *March of the Titans,* Ostara Publications, 2009.

Oppenheimer, S. *The Origins of the British: A Genetic Detective Story.* Constable and Robinson, London, 2006.

Sykes, B. *The Blood of the Isles.* Bantam Press. 2006.

News Sources

"British teacher finds long-lost relative: 9,000-year-old man", The Associated Press, 2008.

"Europe's Ancestors: Cro-Magnon 28,000 Years Old Had DNA Like Modern Humans", *ScienceDaily,* July 16, 2008.

"Origins, age, spread and ethnic association of European haplogroups and subclades", Eupedia, January 2010.

"Tests Reveal Amesbury Archer "King of Stonehenge' Was A Settler From The Alps", *Popular Science,* 2-8-2004

Index

A
Aboriginal Affairs and Reconciliation Division 43
Aboriginal Heritage Act 43
Aboriginal Lands Trust Act 43
Aborigines 43
African Slaves 40
Africans expelled from Britain, 1601 40
Alfred the Great 36
Amazon Indians 46
Amazon rain forests 46
America 5
Amesbury Archer 33
Angles 35
Anglo-Saxons 19, 27, 40
Anglo-Saxon race 36
Atlantic Modal Haplotype 18
Australia 5, 11
Autosomal DNA 10

B
Barrows 32
Basques 29
Belgium 39
Bering Strait 45
Black Sea 21
Boscombe Bowmen 33
Brazil 1, 5, 46
Bristol 40
Bureau of Indian Affairs 45

C
Canute 37
Castlerea 35
Celtic 40
"Celtic" Influence 34
Cheddar Man 31
Clovis culture 46
Columbia 46
Concept of Indigenous Peoples, UN document 3
Creswell Crags 31, 44

D
Danelaw 36
Ddecolonisation 6
Deepcar 31
Deoxyribonucleic acid (DNA) 10
Department of Economic and Social Affairs, UN 3
Draft Declaration on the Rights of Indigenous Peoples 4

E
Ecuador 46
Edward I 39
Edward II 38
English 1, 9
Equality and Human Rights Commission 48
Eric Bloodaxe 36
European Colonisation 5
European-Americans 25

F
Far East 5
Faversham 21
France 39
Franks 35
Frisians 35

G
Genghis Khan 6
Genocide, definition 1
Germany 39
Gough's Cave 31
Guyana 46

H
Han Chinese 6, 44
Haplogroups 10
Harthacnut 38
Hastings, Battle of 38
Hhenges 32
Hengist 37
Hhill forts 32
Horsa 37
Howick 31
Huguenots 40

I
Iberians 29
Indian reservations 5, 45
Indians of North America 45
Indo-European 34
International Labour Organisation Convention 4
Ireland 35
Irish 1, 9
Italians 40

Index

J
Japan 11
Jew 20, 21, 24, 39
Jorvik (York) 36
Jutes 35

L
Liverpool 40
Llangefni 35
Luxembourg 39

M
Māori 42
Mendips 31
Mesolithic Settlement 31
Mexico 5
Mitochondrial DNA (mtDNA) 10
mtDNA Haplotypes Found in Britain 22
Mungo Lake 43
Mungo Man 44
Muslim conquests 6

N
"Nation of immigrants" theory 27
Neolithic period 20
Neolithic Settlement 32
Netherlands 1, 39
New Guinea 11
New South Wales 43
New Zealand 42
Norman Conquest 38
Nubians 6
Nunavut 5

O
Orkney Islands 26
Oronsay 31
Ottoman 6

P
Permanent Forum on Indigenous Issues 3, 42, 46
Persians 6
Peru 46
Phoenicians 20

Q
Queen Elizabeth I 40

R
Red Lady of Paviland 30, 44
Rights of Tribal and Indigenous Peoples, motion 1
Roman s 20, 21
Roman Invasion 35

S
Saxons 35
Scots 1, 9
Short Tandem Repeat 18
Southwell 21
Spain 1
Star Carr 31
Stonehenge 33
Stonehenge Archer 32
Sub-Saharan Africa 5, 11

T
Tibet 6, 44
Torres Strait Islands 43
Trans-Atlantic slave trade 40
Turkic 21

U
United Nations Declaration on the Rights of Indigenous People 7, 48
Upper Palaeolithic Settlement 29
Uttoxeter 21

V
Venezuela 46
Vikings 19
Viking Invasions 36

W
Welsh 1, 9
William the Conqueror 38
World Bank 4

X
X-Chromosomes 10

Y
Y Haplogroup Categories 11
Y-Chromosome Haplotypes Found in Britain 16
Y-chromosomes 10
York 36

Printed in Great Britain
by Amazon.co.uk, Ltd.,
Marston Gate.